WORKING WITH ESSAYS

IT'S ALL ABOUT THE MESSAGE!

WORKING WITH ESSAYS

IT'S ALL ABOUT THE MESSAGE!

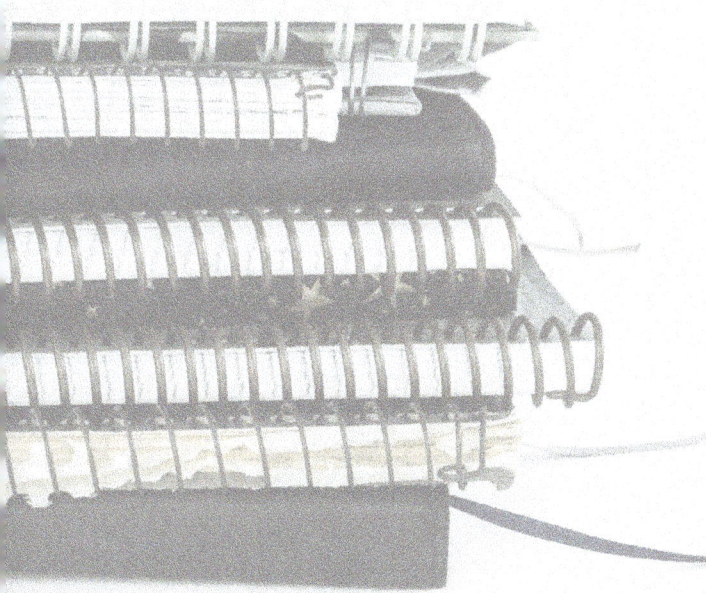

Published by
Heron Books, Inc.
20950 SW Rock Creek Road
Sheridan, OR 97378

heronbooks.com

Special thanks to all the teachers and students who
provided feedback instrumental to this edition.

Second Edition © 2011, 2021 Heron Books
All Rights Reserved

ISBN: 978-0-89-739148-1

Any unauthorized copying, translation, duplication or distribution, in whole or in part, by any means, including electronic copying, storage or transmission, is a violation of applicable laws.

The Heron Books name and the heron bird symbol are registered
trademarks of Delphi Schools, Inc.

Printed in the USA

10 June 2021

At Heron Books, we think learning should be engaging and fun. It should be hands-on and allow students to move at their own pace.

To facilitate this, we have created a learning guide that will help any student progress through this book, chapter by chapter, with confidence and interest.

Get learning guides at
heronbooks.com/learningguides.

For a final exam, email
teacherresources@heronbooks.com

We would love to hear from you!
Email us at *feedback@heronbooks.com.*

Contents

1 AN INTRODUCTION TO THE ESSAY 1

2 THE MESSAGE 5

3 INTEREST 9

4 SUBJECT VS. POINT 13

5 SUPPORTING DETAILS 17

6 BUILDING YOUR ESSAY 21

7 THE PARTS OF AN ESSAY 27

8 OUTLINES 33

9 REVISING 37

10 PROOFREADING 41

11 TYING IT TOGETHER 45

1
AN INTRODUCTION TO THE ESSAY

AN INTRODUCTION TO THE ESSAY

An **essay** is

> a short piece of nonfiction writing on a particular subject.

In school, you have probably been asked to write many essays. As you get older, you will probably be asked to write many more.

When you finish school and begin life as an adult, you will probably find yourself writing proposals, letters, emails, plans and more.

This book focuses only on the basics for writing an essay. Why?

Learning to write a good essay will prepare you well for all the other writing you'll do, in school and in life.

2
THE MESSAGE

THE MESSAGE

When you're writing an essay, you need to have something you want to say.

You need to have a message.

This is the first thing to know about writing an essay—what is your message?

Sometimes it's easy to figure out what your message is. Sometimes it can be harder. Sometimes you are assigned something to write about. But even when it's a required assignment, you need to figure out what *you* want to say—your *message*.

Let's say you are supposed to write about your first day on a sports team. Well, what do you want to say about that first day? Was it horrible? Was there an embarrassing event? Was it the day you found something you are truly passionate about? Was it just an okay day when you thought it was going to be much more exciting? Maybe it was boring because you hate sports? Maybe it was something else. But this all comes back to your *message*. What do *you* want to say about your first day on a sports team?

Once you figure out your message, you can start planning how to get it across to your reader.

3
INTEREST

INTEREST

You know you have to have a message. But what if it's an assignment you aren't that interested in writing about, so you don't have a message *you* want to get across?

When this happens, ask yourself this question:

What about this subject interests me?

There may be some parts of the topic that aren't interesting to you, but usually there is something that *can* be interesting to you. From there, you can start to work out what *you* really think about the topic. You can figure out what part of the topic is important to *you*.

So even when it's an assigned question, you can still work out what *you* want to say within the assignment. And in your essay, you can focus on what is interesting to *you* about the assignment.

Let's see how that might work.

You are assigned to write an essay about dogs, but you think cats would be a much better topic.

Maybe your message is that you think cats are much more interesting than dogs. In your essay you could state many reasons why cats are better than dogs. You're still talking about dogs, just as the assignment asked for. But you have *your* own message, which is that cats really should have been the topic, because they are much more interesting than dogs.

INTEREST

Even when it seems you don't have any choice about an essay, you usually do have a choice. You can choose what you want to say about the topic.

If you choose what's interesting to you and say what you think about that,
the essay is far more likely to be interesting to your reader.

4
SUBJECT VS. POINT

SUBJECT VS. POINT

A **subject** is

a general topic or something you, as a writer, are interested in discussing.

A subject for an essay could be life in China, vacations, chess tournaments, anime, interesting places to visit in New York City, or beatboxing.

A **point** is

the main idea, message, or opinion a writer wants to get across.

The subject is usually general. The point is specific.

As discussed earlier, when you write about a subject but don't have your own message, a point you want to get across, it's not as interesting to the reader. Your teacher, your reader, and others are reading your essay because

they want to know what you have to say.

If they just wanted to learn about life in China, they would research that themselves. Instead, they are reading *your* essay because they want to hear what *your* thoughts are. So make sure when you write an essay about a subject

you first work out what point you want to make.

If the subject is "life in China," then the point might be "Technology is changing life in China faster than ever before." Even this might be too much to cover in a short essay. The point could be narrower and more specific—for example,

SUBJECT VS. POINT

"Chinese people aged 60 and up are using technology in their daily lives more than ever before."

For the subject of vacations, a point might be an opinion, such as, "the best place to go for a vacation is a country you've never visited."

When writing an essay,

start with a subject.
Then find the point you want to make about it.

5
SUPPORTING DETAILS

SUPPORTING DETAILS

You might be asking yourself, "What will help get my message across?"

In writing, **supporting details** are

> additional pieces of information that prove your point.

These help your reader understand your message or point more fully. They help get your message across.

Let's say you want your mom to give you extra spending money for a school trip. How do you convince her? Well, you might tell her that you have been working extra hard. You might add that you want to use the money to buy some special snacks. You might use humor. You might be serious. But if you really want to get your message across, you would give reasons to support your idea.

Here's a rather silly example about a boy named Leo and a girl named Charlotte. Let's see if supporting details help with making a point.

> Leo: "You should go to the dance with me." (That's his point.)

> Charlotte: "I'm not sure. Why do you think I should?" (Charlotte is pretty fearless so she is forcing Leo to explain his point better.)

> Leo: "Well, I am a good date, and I am one of the best dancers in the school. I won the past three school dance-offs." (Now he is giving supporting details.)

SUPPORTING DETAILS

Charlotte: "Well, maybe the part about you being a good dancer is possibly true." (She's still not convinced.)

Leo: "You like horses, right?"

Charlotte: "Yes, but I don't plan to bring a horse to the dance." (She gives him a strange look, since she doesn't know what he is getting at.)

Leo: "Well, what if I told you I have already arranged to pick you up in a horse-drawn carriage?"

Charlotte: "This is starting to get interesting, but I am going to be in a dress and strappy sandals. I'm going to be cold."

Leo: "That's why I have already arranged for extra blankets, with no wool, of course, since you are a vegan. And I will have a thermos with vegan coconut hot chocolate when I pick you up at your door." (He's really supporting his point now.)

Charlotte: "I have to admit. I'm impressed." (His point is definitely getting across.) "I guess I'm going to have to agree after all." (Charlotte responds with a wink because Leo made his point.)

You can see Leo made a plan to get his point across. If he hadn't thought it through and given supporting details, it's unlikely Charlotte would have agreed to go with him.

That was just one somewhat silly example. But it helps show how useful supporting details can be.

With supporting details,
your message is more likely to succeed in getting across.

6
BUILDING YOUR ESSAY

BUILDING YOUR ESSAY

As you know, a sentence is a group of words that expresses a complete thought. A **paragraph** is

> a sentence or a group of sentences that separate
> a longer piece of writing into parts.

A paragraph often tells about one main idea or a part of an idea.

Just as a book is made up of chapters or a movie is made up of scenes, an essay is made up of paragraphs.

Paragraphs, whether long or short, separate what is being talked about into smaller sections. They organize the ideas into groups. Paragraphs make it much easier for the reader to follow the writer's thoughts and get the message.

It is often taught that paragraphs have a beginning, middle and an end. That can be true, but a good paragraph doesn't have to follow that pattern.

Something else that is often taught is the idea that a paragraph has a topic sentence, usually at or toward the beginning. A **topic sentence** is the main sentence that the rest of the paragraph is about.

However, many skilled writers don't pay attention to writing topic sentences. They focus on writing clear paragraphs that work together.

As you continue to read lots of good writing, particularly of writers you enjoy reading, pay attention to the paragraphs. You may find that writers structure their paragraphs in different ways, and you may begin to see what you like and

BUILDING YOUR ESSAY

don't like about how paragraphs are written. The truth is that in the professional world of writing, there aren't strict guidelines on paragraphs as long as they help make the message clear.

What's important is this:

> *paragraphs break a piece of writing into parts so it can stay organized.*

Some Ways of Organizing

There are many ways to organize paragraphs. Here are just a few.

1. Organize them by main thoughts.

   Jonah wanted more allowance. He wanted to use his allowance to save up for new DJ equipment. His plan was to save up enough money to be able to buy DJ equipment by the time the new school year started because he wanted to use it when he DJ'd the homecoming dance at his school. Last school year he had told Mr. Green that the fall homecoming dance would have the best music Crescent High School had ever seen!

   But how could he convince his mom to give him more allowance? He thought and thought and thought about this. He already did all of the yardwork he could do each week. He set the table and did the dishes every night.

   Then he realized what he could do! He could start babysitting his kid sister, Sia. He was old enough now, and he was really good with younger kids. This would be a perfect way to get him to his goal of more allowance to put toward his DJ equipment.

2. Organize them by sequence of events.

   It was a Sunday afternoon and Rocco, the ferret, was acting strange. Sahara started to worry, but her parents said Rocco actually looked fine. She decided to trust them, but she still had a sinking feeling that something was wrong.

BUILDING YOUR ESSAY

By Monday morning, Rocco wasn't moving. He was just lying in his pen. He hadn't eaten his food from last night. That was even more suspicious since he usually ate his food right away. Something was awfully wrong.

Sahara's parents realized she was right and called the veterinarian. The veterinarian told them to bring Rocco in right away.

The veterinarian examined Rocco and found that he had the flu! She gave Sahara exact instructions about what to do to help Rocco heal. Sahara wrote these instructions down so she wouldn't forget them.

She followed the instructions, and within a week, Rocco was back to his normal self again. She was relieved and so, so happy!

From that point forward, Sahara knew she wanted to be a veterinarian.

3. Organize them with reasons that support your message.

    Although Principal Tan has decided chewing gum is no longer allowed in class, we, the students of HK International School, have decided to petition the faculty to change this rule.

    It is true that gum has created a litter problem in the school. There is used chewing gum under tables in classrooms, inside lockers, on the outside of trash cans, and gum has inevitably found its way onto the floor and onto the shoes of faculty and students.

    Luck is in our favor because an exciting development has solved all our problems. Over winter vacation, Stanley Khan created a non-stick gum. This gum is great for chewing, but being non-stick, it won't be able to stick to any of the surfaces that have made it a nuisance.

BUILDING YOUR ESSAY

4. Sometimes making one sentence its own paragraph makes it stand out and have more impact.

   Camping with Odion was more fun than Matteo ever expected. Matteo had no idea that Odion knew how to build a campfire, how to find edible plants in the forest or how to put up a tent in the dark. Although those were important reasons Odion helped make camping fun, they weren't the most important reason. On this particular camping trip, Matteo found out something about Odion he never would have otherwise known.

   Odion could do the most real imitation of a bear any human had ever done before!

   You might be asking, "Why would this make a camping trip fun?" Well, that's just where this story gets interesting.

Things to Keep in Mind

As long as you are organizing your thoughts and breaking up your writing into sections that make sense, you are probably doing a good job with writing paragraphs.

As you continue to write, you'll learn to write better and better paragraphs. That's all part of the process of becoming a better writer. You practice, and you get better and better as you go. Even professional writers keep working to make their writing better.

When you put words together well, you make understandable sentences. When you put sentences together well, you make understandable paragraphs.

When you put paragraphs together well, they add up to writing that gets your message across.

7
THE PARTS OF AN ESSAY

THE PARTS OF AN ESSAY

There are three main parts to an essay. You can probably guess what they are:

the beginning, the middle and the end.

Beginning or Introduction

Since it is *introducing* or opening the writing, sometimes the beginning is called an **introduction**. Introductions can be short or they can be long. They can be a paragraph or a sentence (and anywhere in between). They usually announce the point of the essay.

You want your introduction to get the reader's attention so they are interested in reading the rest of your writing. Other than that, there really aren't any *rules* about an introduction or about what it should say. It just starts the writing off smoothly.

Here are some common ways to write a beginning or introduction:

1. Use a personal detail to get the reader's attention.

   The day I turned sixteen was the strangest day of my life. That was the day I finally got my driver's license. I had no idea what adventure was in store for me.

2. Ask a question. It can be a question to the reader or a question that the essay is going to answer.

   What would happen if our high school, Huxley High, stopped competing in interscholastic sports? Well, the students and faculty at Elon High

THE PARTS OF AN ESSAY

> *School found out the hard answer to that question. Because Huxley High School faculty are now considering the same thing, we need to understand what happened at Elon before moving forward with any plans to end the interscholastic sports program at Huxley.*

3. Use a quotation, statistic, or startling fact.

   Every year, Americans throw away 254 million tons of trash, but only 50% of it can be recycled. We must reduce the amount of non-recyclable trash.

4. Start with something that gives your reader an idea of where you're going.

   Although some people may find hip hop offensive, you can't deny the talent of the great hip hop artists. If you set aside some of the less talented among hip hop artists and really look at the lyrics the great artists write, it's hard to deny what I hope you will come to agree—hip hop artists are important modern-day poets.

The Middle or Body

What follows the beginning or introduction of a piece of writing is the main part. For an essay, this will be most of the paragraphs. This is often called the **body** of the essay.

The paragraphs of the body have most of the details that are doing the work of supporting your point. You want to give enough detailed information for your reader to understand how you reached your conclusion.

It often works well to let the supporting details build up throughout the essay, starting with the weaker supporting details and building to the strongest ones.

The key to the body is to plan the paragraphs so they present ideas that support your point in a logical sequence. This way your reader can follow your reasoning and understand your message.

The Ending or Conclusion

The last sentence or the last paragraph of an essay is often called the **conclusion**. Here conclusion means "an ending." The purpose of the conclusion is to end your writing in a way that ensures your message reached the reader. Often a conclusion summarizes your main message or point.

When you write your conclusion, you want to end the essay smoothly, and you want your reader to feel like everything has been said.

There are many ways to write conclusions that work. Here are a few:

1. Encourage your reader to do something.

   Because honey is important to our health, the cafeteria should provide it for every meal. But the only way this will happen is if you make your voice heard. Contact the Student Council President and tell her, "Honey makes people healthful and happy." Soon we will have honey at every meal.

2. Come back to your introduction and wrap up.

   Whether Elon will have interscholastic sports again remains a question. But I hope the lessons learned there will keep faculty here from ever considering ending interscholastic sports teams at Huxley High School.

3. Leave your reader with something to think about.

   Once we save the honeybees, which are important to our whole ecosystem, we can't stop there. Our environment needs our care and protection. What will you do to help keep the planet safe for the next several generations?

THE PARTS OF AN ESSAY

4. Restate your message in different words.

   Beginning (or introduction): *The most unusual person I ever met was Gryffin Hynds, but he taught me an important lesson about living.*

   Ending (or conclusion): *It has been twenty years, but I won't forget what I learned from Gryffin, because he taught me how to live a happy life. I wonder if there are others out there who learned from Gryffin or if I was the only lucky one.*

Whatever you do to organize your essay, you want to make sure you

get your reader interested,
explain your message with supporting details, and
end the essay clearly and smoothly.

8
OUTLINES

OUTLINES

An **outline** is

> a plan that organizes your ideas so you can get your message across.

It's called an outline because it gives the basic shape of your writing. An outline just has the main points you want to include, not the details.

Think of an outline as a simple tool to help you write an essay. It gets your thoughts in order, helps you keep your point in mind, and organizes your essay into a sequence that works.

If your essay is short, sometimes you won't need to write an outline. You'll still probably want to plan your essay, even if just in your head. But for longer writing, outlines really save time. They keep your ideas straight.

Putting together an outline might involve asking yourself questions to come up with a plan. From there you can write the plan down and then adjust it as needed so it's in an order that makes sense.

These questions can be useful:

> What's the overall point?
>
> Will it answer the question or assignment?
>
> What are the supporting details to make my point?
>
> What's the best way to organize all these ideas?

OUTLINES

What's the best way to start the essay?

What's the best way to end it?

When you are working on an essay, you may have more ideas that come to mind. Writers often do. If you get a new idea about the essay while you're writing it, you can add it into the outline. This can help you get the new idea into the essay in a logical place, rather than just sticking it in wherever it might not belong. By revising your outline, you can keep track of these ideas and keep your message clear.

Outlines are a simple and useful tool.
Use them to organize your thoughts and get your message across clearly.

9
REVISING

REVISING

Once you've finished writing your essay, you'll want to read it over.

You'll want to see if it is organized well, makes sense, and gets your message across.

Sometimes you can finish writing an essay and discover it may not actually say everything you wanted to say in the way you meant to say it.

It may have some confusing paragraphs or paragraphs that don't flow from one to the next. It may have information you now realize isn't needed, or it may be missing information you now realize you really do need to include.

One of the hardest things to do is to freshly look at your writing as if you were a reader. You have to step into your reader's shoes and see if he or she can get your message by reading your essay exactly as you wrote it. If you can look at your own writing freshly, you'll be able to see whether your message gets across.

Some people use a checklist of things to look for in a completed piece of writing. You can write your own or use something like this:

1. Does each sentence say what I meant?
2. Do the paragraphs say what I meant?
3. Do I have enough supporting details?
4. Do the paragraphs fit together well?
5. Did I leave out anything important?
6. Did I include anything that doesn't really add to my message?
7. Does my message get across?

REVISING

However you decide to review your writing, what is most important is that you

look at the writing freshly to see if your message comes across.

If it doesn't, you can revise your essay so it does. Generally, writers review and revise their writing as much as needed until they are confident their message is clear.

10 PROOFREADING

PROOFREADING

Mistakes in pieces of writing can block someone's understanding of the message. If you read something that has misspelled words or incorrect sentences, it can be hard to understand or less enjoyable to read.

Proofreading is

>reading over writing to catch errors.

You may need to proofread a paper more than once. However many times it takes, you'll want to catch all the errors—misspellings, poor punctuation and typos.

Just as with revising, people often have their own preferred way of proofreading. Some like to print out their writing because that makes it easier for them to spot errors. Others like to read it out loud. Some read their paper backwards for spelling errors.

How you do it really doesn't matter as much as just doing it. With all the work you put in to make your writing clear, you don't want to let errors stop the reader from getting your message!

Proofreading is a skill all writers have to work to get better at. With practice, you'll get better at catching your errors so your message comes across without distractions.

11
TYING IT TOGETHER

TYING IT TOGETHER

Here are some final tips. Some of these are a review, but there are a few new tips to help you on your way:

1. Build on the skills you already have as a writer by reading good books, articles, essays, stories—any good writing.

2. Make sure you figure out what *you* want to say.

3. Follow any advice on writing that helps you write more clearly. If it doesn't, it's probably not good advice.

4. Write. Write a lot.

5. Make sure your writing gets its intended message across. Revise your writing until your message is clear.

6. Get other people to read what you wrote. Sometimes this will be a teacher and sometimes a friend or even a family member.

7. Experiment. Try new things. Be willing to make new mistakes and learn from them. And whatever you do when working with essays, remember this:

It's all about the message!

www.ingramcontent.com/pod-product-compliance
Lightning Source LLC
Chambersburg PA
CBHW050504110426
42742CB00018B/3371